You Can Draw

ANIMALS

Jordan McGill

Step 1
Go to **www.av2books.com**

Step 2
Enter this unique code

JDYRFIBVE

Step 3
Explore your interactive eBook!

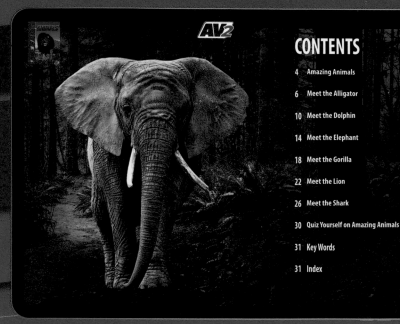

CONTENTS

AV2 is optimized for use on any device

Your interactive eBook comes with...

Contents
Browse a live contents page to easily navigate through resources

Audio
Listen to sections of the book read aloud

Videos
Watch informative video clips

Weblinks
Gain additional information for research

Try This!
Complete activities and hands-on experiments

Key Words
Study vocabulary, and complete a matching word activity

Quizzes
Test your knowledge

Slideshows
View images and captions

... and much, much more!

CONTENTS

AMAZING ANIMALS

Incredible animals that defy belief live in all parts of the world. These animals find everything they need to survive in their environment. In nature, they live best without interference from humans. They have **adapted** to be very successful in their environments. Some animals, such as the shark, have lived successfully for millions of years.

WHY DRAW?

triangles

Drawing animals is a great way to learn more about them. You can learn about the features they have and how these features make them successful in their environment. You can also consider how the animal would survive without these features.

Look around you. The world is made of shapes and lines. By combining simple shapes and lines, anything can be drawn. A fox's ear is just a triangle with a few details added. A panda's head can be a circle. Almost anything, no matter how complicated, can be broken down into simple shapes.

circle

What shapes do you see in this hippopotamus?

Meet the
ALLIGATOR

Alligators belong to a group of animals called reptiles. Reptiles have hard, scaly skin all over their bodies. Snakes, lizards, and turtles are also reptiles.

Alligators spend part of their time on land and part of their time in rivers or lakes. They are expert swimmers. Alligators stay near the surface of the water so that they can breathe air.

Eyes
Alligators have good eyesight and can see well underwater. They have a clear eyelid that covers their eyes underwater. This allows them to see underwater without irritation.

Nostrils
Nostrils on top of the alligator's head let the animal breathe while it hides underwater.

Jaws
Alligators have very sharp teeth for catching and eating **prey**. Alligators eat only meat.

YOU CAN DRAW

Plates
Tough, scaly skin protects the alligator from other animals.

Tail
An alligator pushes itself through the water with its strong tail. Sometimes, an alligator will use its tail to knock other animals down.

Claws
Alligators have five claws on each front foot and four claws on each back foot. They have webbing between their claws. This helps them swim.

How to Draw an
ALLIGATOR

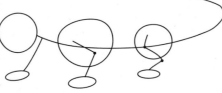

(1) Start with a simple stick figure of the alligator. Use circles for the head and body, ovals for the feet, and lines for the limbs and tail.

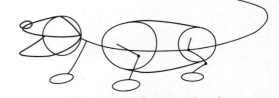

(2) Now, join the two body circles together with a smooth, curved line. Then, draw the jaws and a small circle on the tip of the upper jaw. This will become the alligator's **snout**.

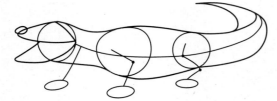

(3) Next, join the circles for the head and body with curved lines, and draw the tail around the tail line.

(4) In this step, draw the legs and tongue, as shown.

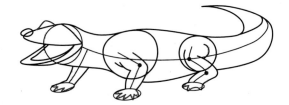

5 Next, draw the webbed paws and a lump on the head, which is the eye on the other side.

6 Draw the other eye and teeth. Then, draw scales on the body and tail using small curved lines.

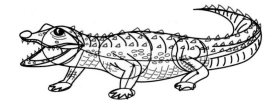

7 Draw lumps on the back and tail, and add checkered lines on the belly for scales.

8 Erase the extra lines and the stick figure frame.

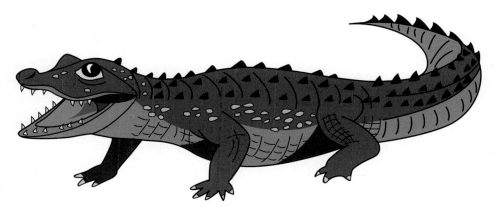

9 Color the picture.

Meet the
DOLPHIN

Dolphins are friendly and smart animals that always seem to be smiling. They live in natural bodies of water around the world.

Many people confuse dolphins with fish. Dolphins are **marine mammals**. They breathe air just like humans. A dolphin rises to the surface of the ocean every few minutes to breathe through a blowhole on top of its head.

240
The approximate number of teeth the long-beaked common dolphin has.

Up to 30
The height, in feet, that dolphins can jump out of the water. (9.1 meters)

Blowhole
The blowhole is used for breathing. Dolphins keep the blowhole shut when underwater. They only open it to breathe.

Beak
Inside a dolphin's beak are teeth. A dolphin's teeth are cone-shaped with sharp points. They are used to grab and hold on to food.

Dorsal Fin
The dorsal fin helps keep the dolphin balanced.

Tail
The tail moves up and down. It helps the dolphin swim.

Flippers
Flippers are used to steer the dolphin through water.

Melon
The melon, located on the forehead, helps send underwater sounds.

How to Draw a
DOLPHIN

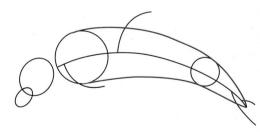

1 Start with a simple stick figure of the dolphin. Use circles for the body, ovals for the snout and head, and lines for the fins.

2 Now, join the two body circles together with a smooth, curved line in the shape of a curved teardrop.

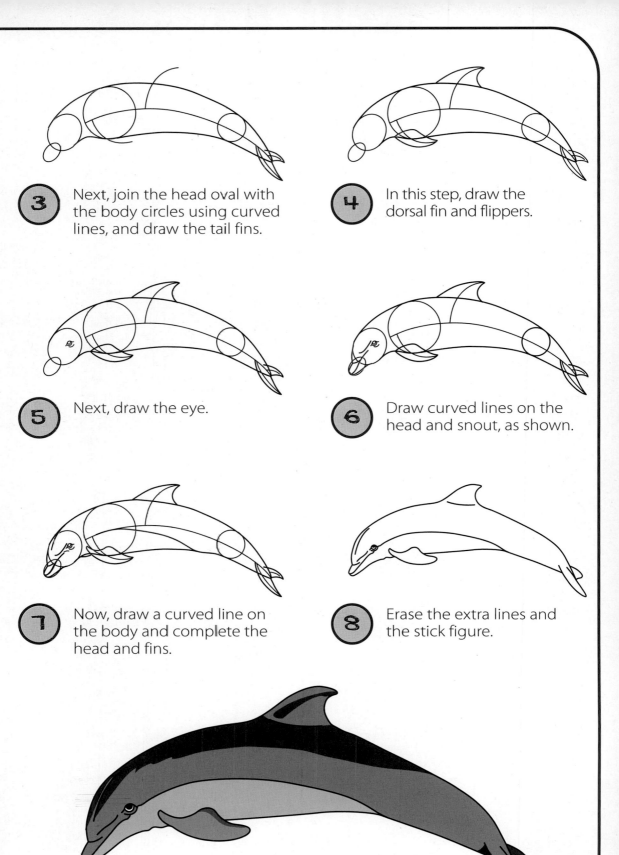

3 Next, join the head oval with the body circles using curved lines, and draw the tail fins.

4 In this step, draw the dorsal fin and flippers.

5 Next, draw the eye.

6 Draw curved lines on the head and snout, as shown.

7 Now, draw a curved line on the body and complete the head and fins.

8 Erase the extra lines and the stick figure.

9 Color the picture.

Meet the
ELEPHANT

The elephant is the largest animal that lives on land. It has a huge, bulky body and a long nose called a trunk. Two curved tusks grow on either side of the trunk. Tusks are long, sharp teeth. They are made of a hard material called **ivory**.

Tusks
Sharp tusks are useful for digging up plants to eat.

22,928
The weight, in pounds, of the largest elephant ever recorded. (10,400 kilograms)

12 to 18
The number of hours an elephant spends eating every day.

Trunk
A trunk can make a loud noise like a trumpet to call other elephants. To drink, an elephant sucks up water with its trunk. Then, it sprays the water into its mouth.

14 YOU CAN DRAW

Ears
An elephant flaps its large ears to keep itself cool.

Skin
Thick skin protects the elephant from thorns and stinging insects. The wrinkles keep the elephant cool by trapping moisture in the folds.

Legs
Strong legs with wide feet support the elephant's body.

How to Draw an
ELEPHANT

① Start with a simple stick figure of the elephant. Use a circle for the body, ovals for the head and trunk, and lines for the limbs.

② Now, join the head oval and body circle with a smooth, curved line. Draw the trunk with curved lines, as shown.

YOU CAN DRAW

3 Next, draw the legs.

4 In this step, draw the eyes and tail.

5 Then, draw the ears.

6 Now, draw the tusks and nails.

7 Draw curved lines on the head, body, and ears for the wrinkles. Then, draw hair on the tail.

8 Erase the extra lines and the stick figure frame.

9 Color the picture.

Meet the
GORILLA

Gorillas are big, strong, intelligent animals. They live in the forests of West and Central Africa. Gorillas are the largest members of the great ape family.

Most people think that gorillas are scary animals. Gorillas are very calm, peaceful, and kind. These big, fearsome-looking animals are **herbivores**.

Face
Gorillas have no hair on their faces. Each gorilla has its own unique facial features.

Nose
Gorillas have distinct noses. Researchers can tell one gorilla from another by the shape of its nose.

8.5
Approximate width, in feet, that a gorilla's arm span can reach. (2.6 m)

40
The amount of food a male gorilla can eat in a day, in pounds. (18 kg)

Hands
Gorilla hands have four fingers and an **opposable** thumb. Gorillas use their hands to eat. They mostly eat plants.

Head Crest
Gorillas have a bulging forehead called a crest.

Chest
Their wide chest makes gorillas appear huge. Gorillas beat their chest when they are excited, angry, or frightened.

Feet
Gorilla feet have five toes. The big toe is opposable.

How to Draw a
GORILLA

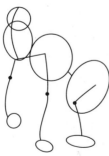

1 Start with a simple stick figure of the gorilla. Use ovals for the head, hands, feet, and body. Use lines for the limbs.

2 Now, join the head and body ovals together with curved lines. Draw curved lines on the face, as shown.

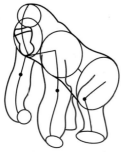

3 Next, draw the arms and legs.

4 In this step, draw the hands and feet.

5 Then, draw the nose, mouth, ear, and nails.

6 Now, draw the eyes.

7 Draw hair on the head, body, and limbs.

8 Erase the extra lines and the stick figure frame.

9 Color the picture.

Meet the
LION

A lion is a large animal with four strong legs and sharp teeth. A female lion is called a lioness. Lions are **mammals**, which are animals that feed their babies milk and have hair or fur on their bodies.

Lions belong to the same family as pet cats, but a person could not keep a mighty lion as a pet. It is one of the fiercest **predators** on Earth.

Eyes
A lion's large eyes help it to see well at night.

Paws
A lion's huge paws have soft pads that help the animal move quietly while hunting.

Mane

A mane is the thick hair that covers much of a lion's head and upper body. The shaggy mane protects the lion's neck against attacks by other lions.

Jaws

Lions' powerful jaws and long, pointed teeth are used for killing other animals. A lion may eat 70 pounds (32 kg) of meat in one meal. That is the same as eating 280 large hamburgers.

Back Claws

Lions' back paws have four sharp claws. A lion's claws can be 3 inches (7.6 cm) long.

① Start with a simple stick figure of the lion. Use circles for the head and body, ovals for the snout and feet, and lines for the limbs and tail.

② Now, join the two body circles together with a smooth, curved line. Draw a large circle around the head. This will become the lion's mane.

3 Next, draw the ears and mouth.

4 In this step, draw the legs, as shown.

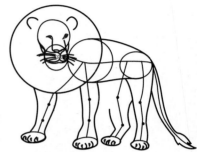

5 Then, draw the tail and paws.

6 Now, draw the eyes, nose, whiskers, and nails.

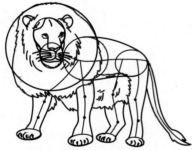

7 Draw the mane and hair around the head, body, and tail.

8 Erase the extra lines and the stick figure frame.

9 Color the picture.

Meet the
SHARK

Great white sharks are large, meat-eating fish. They are the most dangerous of all sharks.

The great white shark's skin is covered with a layer of tiny teeth called **denticles**. These denticles make the shark's skin feel like sandpaper.

Snout
A shark's snout is used to smell, but not to breathe. The great white shark can smell one drop of blood in 25 gallons (95 liters) of water.

35,000
The approximate number of teeth a sandbar shark will have over its lifetime.

59
The length, in feet, a whale shark, the world's largest fish, can grow to be. (18 meters)

Teeth
Sharks have sharp teeth and huge jaws. Great white sharks tear their food into mouth-sized pieces that they swallow whole.

Gill Slits
Gills are used for breathing.

Dorsal Fin
The dorsal fin helps the shark keep its balance.

Tail
Great white sharks have a tail shaped like a moon.

Pectoral Fins
Pectoral fins on both sides of a shark's body control direction of movement.

How to Draw a
SHARK

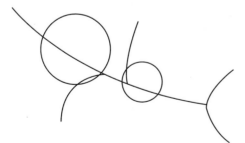

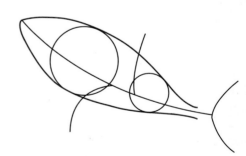

1 Start by drawing a stick figure of the shark. Use circles for the head and body, and lines for the fins.

2 Now, join the two body circles together with smooth, curved lines, starting from tip of the central line and ending before the tail fin.

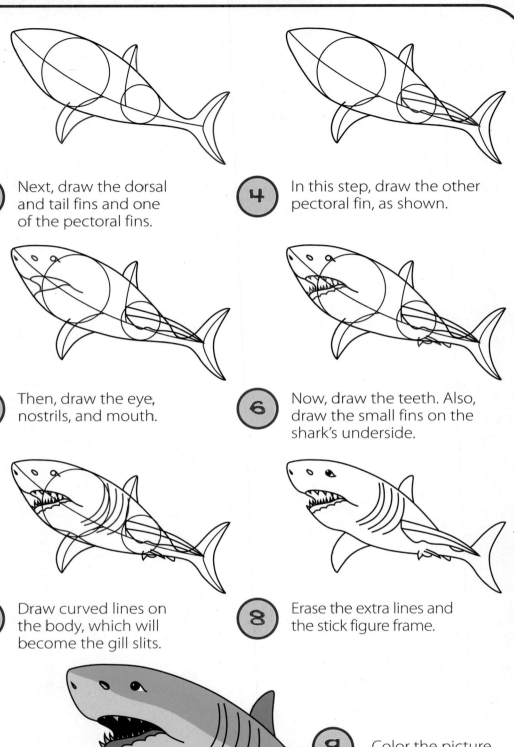

3 Next, draw the dorsal and tail fins and one of the pectoral fins.

4 In this step, draw the other pectoral fin, as shown.

5 Then, draw the eye, nostrils, and mouth.

6 Now, draw the teeth. Also, draw the small fins on the shark's underside.

7 Draw curved lines on the body, which will become the gill slits.

8 Erase the extra lines and the stick figure frame.

9 Color the picture.

Quiz Yourself on AMAZING ANIMALS

01 To what group of animals do alligators belong?

02 Are dolphins fish?

03 What material are an elephant's tusks made of?

04 What do gorillas usually eat?

05 How large are lions' claws?

06 What is a shark's snout used for?

07 What part of a dolphin helps keep it balanced?

08 How many hours per day does an elephant spend eating?

09 Where do gorillas live in nature?

10 What is the largest type of fish in the world?

ANSWER
01 Reptiles. 02 No. Dolphins are marine mammals. 03 Ivory 04 Plants 05 A lion's claws can be 3 inches (7.6 cm) long. 06 To smell 07 Dorsal fin 08 12 to 18 09 West and Central Africa 10 Whale shark.

YOU CAN DRAW

KEY WORDS

adapted: changed appearance or behavior over time to fit into a living environment

denticles: small teeth or toothlike structures

herbivores: animals that eat plants

ivory: the hard, white substance that makes up the tusks of animals such as elephants, walruses, and narwhals

mammals: animals that have fur, make milk, and are born live

marine mammals: warm-blooded animals that live in water

nostrils: openings on the nose that admit air and scents

opposable: the ability to place the first finger and the thumb together to grasp things

predators: animals that hunt other animals for food

prey: an animal that is hunted for food

snout: the projecting nose and mouth of an animal

INDEX

Get the best of both worlds.

AV2 bridges the gap between print and digital.

The expandable resources toolbar enables quick access to content including **videos**, **audio**, **activities**, **weblinks**, **slideshows**, **quizzes**, and **key words**.

Animated videos make static images come alive.

Resource icons on each page help readers to further **explore key concepts**.

Published by AV2
350 5th Avenue, 59th Floor
New York, NY 10118
Website: www.av2books.com

Library of Congress Cataloging-in-Publication Data
Names: McGill, Jordan.
Title: You can draw animals / Jordan McGill.
Description: New York : AV2, [2021] | Includes index. | Audience: Ages 10-12 | Audience: Grades 4-6
Identifiers: LCCN 2019050531 (print) | LCCN 2019050532 (ebook) | ISBN 9781791119799 (library binding) | ISBN 9781791119805 (paperback) | ISBN 9781791119812 | ISBN 9781791119829
Subjects: LCSH: Animals in art. | Drawing--Technique--Juvenile literature.
Classification: LCC NC780 .A46 2021 (print) | LCC NC780 (ebook) | DDC 743.6--dc23
LC record available at https://lccn.loc.gov/2019050531
LC ebook record available at https://lccn.loc.gov/2019050532

Printed in Guangzhou, China
1 2 3 4 5 6 7 8 9 0 24 23 22 21 20

042020
101319

Project Coordinator: Heather Kissock
Designer: Terry Paulhus